I LIVE WITH DOWN SYNDROME

WRITTEN BY CHRISTINA EARLEY

ILLUSTRATED BY
AMANDA HUDSON

A Starfish Book

SEAHORSE
PUBLISHING

Teaching Tips for Caregivers:

As a caregiver, you can help your child succeed in school by giving them a strong foundation in language and literacy skills and a desire to learn to read.

This book helps children grow by letting them practice reading skills.

Reading for pleasure and interest will help your child to develop reading skills and will give your child the opportunity to practice these skills in meaningful ways.

- Encourage your child to read on her own at home
- Encourage your child to practice reading aloud
- Encourage activities that require reading
- Establish a reading time
- Talk with your child
- Give your child writing materials

Teaching Tips for Teachers:

Research shows that one of the best ways for students to learn a new topic is to read about it.

Before Reading

- Read the "Words to Know" and discuss the meaning of each word.
- Read the back cover to see what the book is about.

During Reading

- When a student gets to a word that is unknown, ask them to look at the rest of the sentence to find clues to help with the meaning of the unknown word.
- Ask the student to write down any pages of the book that were confusing to them.

After Reading

- Discuss the main idea of the book.
- Ask students to give one detail that they learned in the book by showing a text dependent answer from the book.

TABLE OF CONTENTS

I LIVE WITH DOWN SYNDROME

Hi! My name is Cecilia.

I am eight years old.

I live with my mom, dad, and older sister Joy. I have a dog named Max.

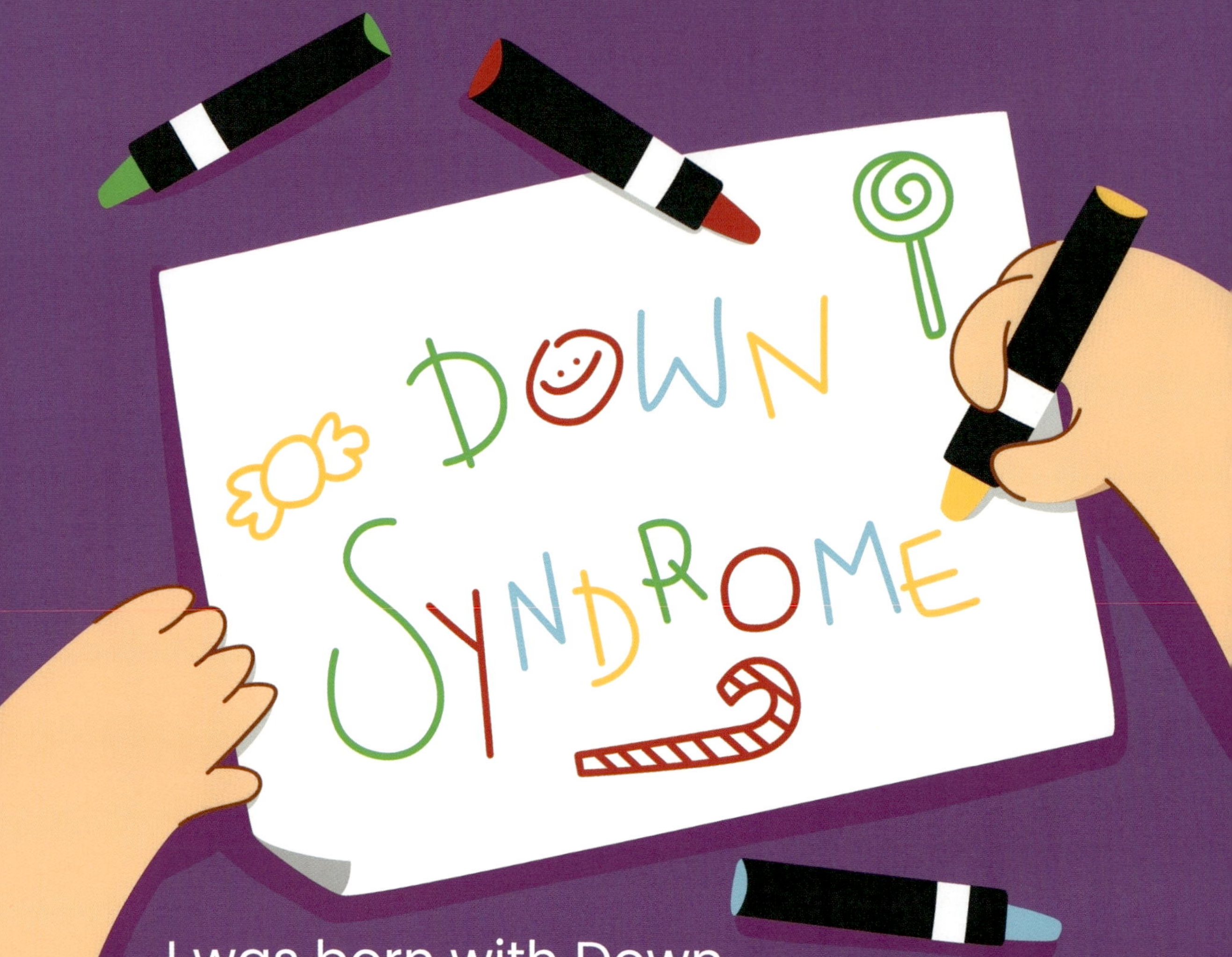

I was born with Down syndrome. I learn new things at my own **pace**.

It is hard for me to speak clearly. Sometimes, I use a special **device** that talks for me.

Most people have 46 **chromosomes** that make them who they are.

I have one extra copy of chromosome number 21. So, I have 47 chromosomes!

I ride the bus to school.

I sit next to my friend Maria.

We both have unicorn backpacks!

A chart with pictures is on my desk.
It reminds me what I need to do.

Mr. Lee helps me **practice** my reading with my friend Bruce. It is hard, but I know I can be a great reader!

I carry my lunch tray to the table.
Toby peels my apple for me.

Today's special is music. I have to **concentrate** to follow the hand motions.

I like to bake cupcakes. I put sprinkles on top to make them fancy.

I would like to own a bakery when I grow up. What do you want to do when you grow up?

LEARN ABOUT DOWN SYNDROME

What Is Down Syndrome?

Down syndrome is a condition in which a person is born with an extra chromosome. Chromosomes are thread-like structures in each cell of the human body. They are made of genes that provide the information that determines everything about a person, such as hair color or height. Most people are born with 23 pairs of chromosomes, or 46 in all. The extra genetic material that a person with Down syndrome has can cause problems with how their bodies develop and learn things.

People with Down syndrome can have flattened faces with almond-shaped eyes that slant upward. They can have smaller ears, hands, and feet. Babies born with Down syndrome reach milestones, such as walking, talking, and eating, at a slower pace. At school, they will need special help to learn and communicate.

As adults, people with Down syndrome have jobs and families. With the support of the community, they can lead typical lives.

Websites to Visit

National Association for Down Syndrome: nads.org

National Down Syndrome Congress: ndsccenter.org

National Down Syndrome Society: ndss.org

The Arc: thearc.org

Take the Pledge for Inclusion

- ☑ I accept people of all abilities.
- ☑ I respect others and act with kindness and compassion.
- ☑ I include people with special needs and disabilities in my school and in my community.

Get your parent's permission to sign the online pledge at PledgeforInclusion.org.

Celebrate and Educate

World Down Syndrome Day is March 21st.

Down Syndrome Month happens in October.

Inclusive Schools Week is the first full week in December.

Famous People with Down Syndrome

Sujeet Desai: First musician with Down syndrome to play at Carnegie Hall

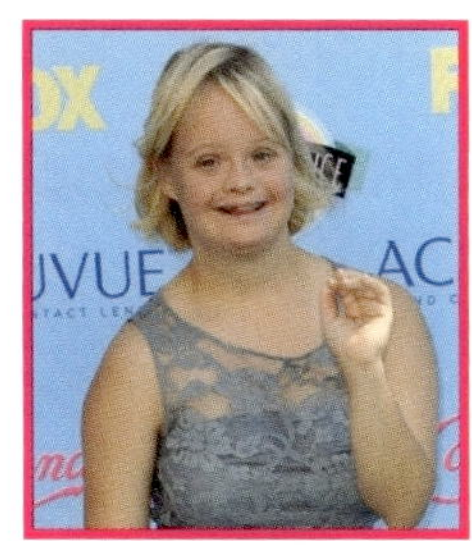

Lauren Potter

Collette Divitto: Entrepreneur and founder of Collettey's Cookies

Chris Nikic: First person with Down syndrome to complete an Ironman triathlon

Pablo Pineda: First European with Down syndrome to get a college degree

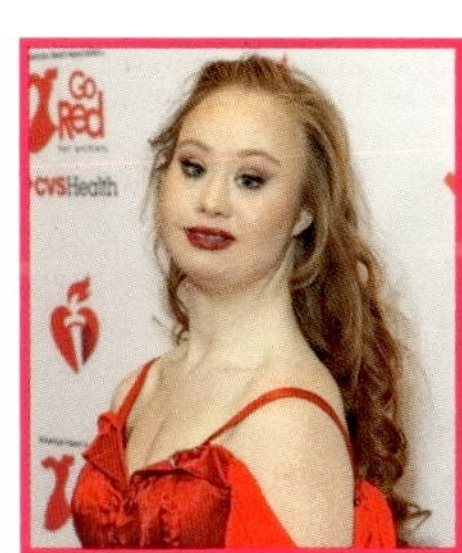

Madeline Stuart

Lauren Potter: Actress in television show *Glee*

Madeline Stuart: Fashion designer and founder of clothing line 21 Reasons Why

WORDS TO KNOW

chromosomes (KRO-muh-sohmz): tiny structures inside the cells that make up living things

concentrate (KAHN-suhn-trate): to focus

device (DI-vise): a machine such as a tablet

pace (pase): a rate of speed

practice (PRAK-tis): do regularly to improve

INDEX

COMPREHENSION QUESTIONS

1. What is on Cecilia's desk to help her?

a. a book

b. a chart

c. a clock

2. How does Cecilia get to school?

a. by bus

b. by car

c. by bike

3. Who peels the apple at lunch for Cecilia?

a. Marco

b. Toby

c. Joy

4. True or False: Most people have 46 chromosomes.

5. True or False: Cecilia sometimes uses a special device to help her talk.

Answers: 1. b, 2. a, 3. b, 4. True, 5. True

ABOUT THE AUTHOR

Christina Earley lives in sunny south Florida with her son, husband, and rescue dog. She has been teaching children with special needs for over 25 years. She loves to bake cookies, read books about animals, and ride roller coasters.

Written by: Christina Earley
Illustrated by: Amanda Hudson
Design by: Under the Oaks Media
Editor: Kim Thompson

Photos: Featureflash Photo Agency/Shutterstock: p. 21 (Lauren Potter); lev radin/Shutterstock: p. 21 (Madeline Stuart)

Library of Congress PCN Data
I Live with Down Syndrome /Christina Earley
I Live With
ISBN 979-8-8873-5345-6(hard cover)
ISBN 979-8-8873-5430-9(paperback)
ISBN 979-8-8873-5515-3(EPUB)
ISBN 979-8-8873-5600-6(eBook)
Library of Congress Control Number: 2022948898

Printed in the United States of America.

Seahorse Publishing Company
www.seahorsepub.com

Published in the United States
Seahorse Publishing
PO Box 771325
Coral Springs, FL 33077